I0816027

KRUGER SAFARI

Gerald Hinde & Will Taylor

HPH Publishing

To the brave and tireless anti-poaching units
who stand guard in the war for the survival of wildlife,
your unwavering dedication, courage and sacrifice
in the face of danger serve as a beacon of hope
for all threatened creatures.

Your efforts and determination to protect
and preserve these populations are commendable
and crucial to the survival of many species.
They are a testament to the strength of
the human spirit and the profound respect for life.

This book honours your relentless fight
and the extraordinary work you do daily.
While your efforts encompass the protection of various species,
we especially recognise the critical role you play in rhino anti-poaching.

Your dedication ensures future generations can witness
the beauty and majesty of these animals in the wild,
a legacy that will endure for years to come

With deepest gratitude and admiration.

Gerald Hinde and Will Taylor

CONTENTS

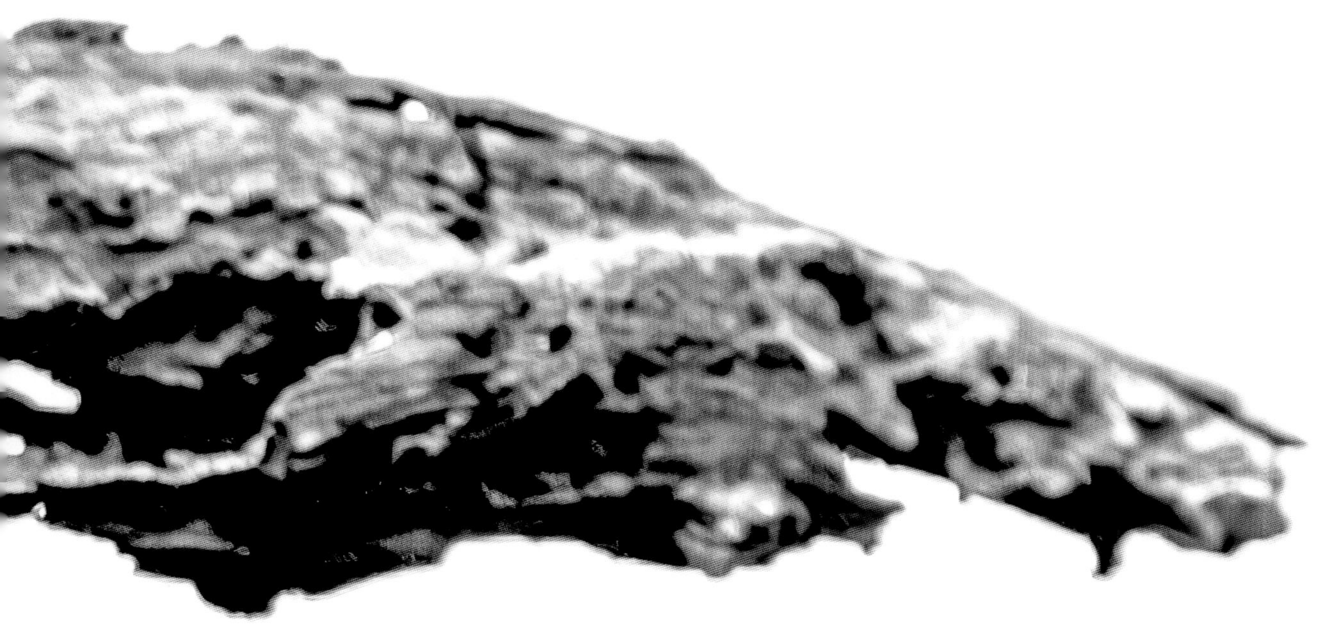

INTRODUCTION

The Kruger National Park is one of the world's most iconic and important national parks, and is a globally recognised conservation area. It has a rich history filled with stories of intrepid men, incredible animals and a legacy of conservation successes (and a few failures) that make up the fabric from which this incredible place is woven. It owes its existence to a few visionary individuals, who saw the prospect of a decline in animals and habitats owing to unregulated hunting and encroachment of human activities, as a deep threat to this formerly pristine wilderness.

The Kruger is vast by any measure – roughly 360 km long, and 40 to 80 km wide – covering an area of approximately 19 500 square kilometres or nearly two million acres!

Since becoming South Africa's first national park in 1923, millions of visitors, over more than a hundred years, have memories of time spent in this magical wilderness, and stories of amazing interactions with, and observations of, animals in their natural habitat.

While both Gerald and I have spent countless hours in Kruger, and still enjoy our visits there, our attention over the last 30 years or so has been focused on the areas to the west of the park, which together with the park itself has become known as the Greater Kruger National Park.

This area is made up of around 3 500 square kilometres of land that is variously owned privately, or by local communities, and has become a deeply important part of the entire area's conservation success. We will go briefly into the history of the various areas later in the book, but essentially these were freehold 'farms' that were used by their owners over the years for hunting, livestock farming and general recreation. They were fenced off from the park but the landowners got together and, over time, formed their own private nature reserves. The first of these was the Sabi Sand Wildtuin, or Sabi Sand Game Reserve, which came into being in 1948. The 50 km fence between the Kruger and the Sabi Sand came down in 1993 and over the next few years, almost all of the private reserves on the west truly became a functioning part of the Greater Kruger.

This was a vitally important move because the elongated north/west-oriented shape of the Kruger allowed for the movement of animals only up and down the reserve, whereas the ancient seasonal migration pathways of the animals in this area ran in an east-west direction, from the low-lying coastal areas of Mozambique in the east, to the slopes and foothills of the Drakensberg mountains in the west. The gradual movement of the fence to the west, and the continued incorporation of more and more land whose owners and communities started to see the value of wildlife tourism, began to open up access to some of these original movement routes.

Historically a lot of these farms to the west of the park were hunting areas; unfortunately, predator species were quite heavily targeted as there were numerous attempts at cattle and livestock farming, and all the predator species were classed as vermin. Lion, leopard, hyena, jackal and even wild dogs were killed with impunity, and their numbers dwindled drastically. Other species were shot for the pot and, in later years, the Big Five were targeted as trophies.

A few of the land owners began to recognise the importance of game viewing as a pastime and source of income, and operations such as MalaMala Game Reserve introduced this as an option for visitors, slowly moving away from hunting to pure non-extractive use of the land and its wildlife.

By the late 1970s, the concept of the 'private' game reserve had firmly taken hold and extensive land was falling under stewardship that concentrated entirely on photographic rather than hunting safaris. This was the beginning of the highly sophisticated and world-class tourist offering that makes up the Greater Kruger National Park. International visitors became familiar with the quality of both the hospitality operation, and the incredible game-viewing opportunities presented by the private reserves. Here you were able to head out on game drive in an open vehicle with a trained ranger and tracker and actively track and find the most sought-after game species. You were able to follow animals off-road and enjoy night game drives with a spot light, which opened up a whole new world. It was a paradigm shift in game viewing on the continent and, by the time South Africa truly opened up to the rest of the world after independence in 1994, the reputation of the Kruger Park and surrounds was set.

Separately, Gerald and I started visiting the Kruger National Park and the Sabi Sand Nature Reserve in the mid 1980s. I began working at MalaMala while he was photographing leopards on some of the neighbouring properties for his then current project. This was (and still is) without a doubt the best place in the world to see this elusive spotted cat, and both of us independently developed a love for leopards that culminated in our meeting, which is well chronicled in our other books.

As populations of animals became more secure and relaxed in the presence of game-viewing vehicles, the opportunities to get deeply into the lives of species such as lion, leopard and elephant became more possible. In the private game reserves, the vehicle has become a sort of magic carpet on which you are able to enter into the life of these animals in a completely neutral way. Generations of leopard and lion cubs have grown up around vehicles, and regard them as they would any other object that does not affect their lives, either positively or negatively. Early on in the pioneering of game viewing from open vehicles, we developed a strict set of rules by which rangers operated, to ensure the comfort and security of the animals and the safety of guests. All of this has led to a mutual trust, while still bearing in mind these are wild animals and are always to be approached with caution.

In this book, we decided to concentrate largely on the photographic aspect of all these years of experiences and allow the pictures to evoke the feeling of these interactions, while allowing the words to give some context, tell the stories and describe the sense of place.

We hope you enjoy this book. We are so honoured to be able to share the rare privilege we have had in being a part of the evolution of the Greater Kruger Park.

A SENSE OF PLACE
THE GREATER KRUGER NATIONAL PARK

Across the vastness of the African continent, there is a myriad array of habitats and wilderness areas that are overwhelming in the scope of their diversity and difference. If we imagine looking at the continent from space and slowly zooming in, we see these patches of green and brown and blue, all distinct and detached, where they all used to be conjoined and continuous. The impact of man and his ability to change the environment has caused these distinct ecosystems to slowly contract and shrink into islands separated by a sea of human encroachment. Each of these distinct systems is deeply important; tropical rain forest, freshwater lakes and wetlands, vast sand deserts, high montane plateau, and miles and miles of rolling grassland savanna. Each supports important and unique systems and species, from the tiniest insects to herds of megafauna – and every individual of every species is a vital piece of a giant web of interactions.

For lovers of nature, wildlife and wild places, Africa is overwhelming. There is so much to see! So many places with so many fascinating landscapes and creatures. Each of us is drawn to different types of habitats and find ourselves at home and happiest in a variety of environments, and some of these places are so special that you feel it as soon as you arrive. For some, it is the mountains, for others, the lakes, rivers and oceans ... but you know it when you feel it. Your soul tells you that this is where I am at my happiest.

I call this a sense of place – and over the last 30 or 40 years, Gerald and I have been privileged enough to have this feeling about the mixed woodland and savannas of the southern African subcontinent in general, and the Greater Kruger Park in particular. I have seen that satisfied smile spread over the faces of visitors from all over the world, as they slowly leave behind the burdens and noise of civilisation and head out on their first game drive, in an open vehicle, in this special place we call 'the bush'.

As mentioned in the introduction, the Greater Kruger refers to the approximately 3 500 square kilometres of protected land to the west of Kruger National Park, an area that has been growing steadily over the years, as more and more private and local community land owners are included. This has provided an important extension of habitat available to conservation efforts, as well as an extremely important increase in income for the further protection of this vital piece of South Africa's environmental heritage.

The Greater Kruger is utilised primarily for photographic tourism and is home to some of South Africa's best-known luxury safari lodges. Relatively high prices and strict access control result in low visitor numbers compared to the neighbouring KNP. The commercialisation of these areas has generated significant income from tourist dollars to go towards conservation and anti-poaching efforts, as well as providing stimulus for local economies and employment opportunities.

A brief history

It is only really possible to give a short overview of the history of the Greater Kruger, as each area has its own unique – and sometimes convoluted – history.

Essentially, most of the properties adjoining the Kruger Park to the west were either hunting or farming and ranching areas. They were privately owned by individuals, companies or local communities. There was little thought given to conservation in those early days, and any wildlife that conflicted with the use of the land was quickly eradicated.

Shortly before the Boer War in the late 1800s, the president of the Republic Of South Africa was Stephanus Johannes Paulus Kruger – better known by the world as Paul Kruger. Kruger was the first to recognise that the wild parts of South Africa needed immediate attention if they were to survive the depredations of hunting, mining and farming, and to stay, as he put it, "where nature could remain unspoilt as the Creator made it". After introducing new game laws protecting certain species in 1891, it was not until 1898 that he managed to have the Government's Reserve proclaimed – the area between the Sabie and Crocodile rivers – as the Sabi Nature Reserve.

Enter one James Stevenson-Hamilton, an Irishman who had, until this point, lived an incredibly active and interesting life as a soldier in the British Army and consummate adventurer and explorer. He was from a wealthy family, a bachelor, and a steadfast conservationist, who was deemed perfect for the job of warden of the Sabi Nature Reserve by Sir Godfrey Lagden, who was the newly appointed Commissioner of Native Affairs.

Stevenson-Hamilton took on this new idea of game ranging with gusto, and through incredible adversity and with sheer grit, halted the shooting of animals and began the process of restoring the land to nature. His powerful will and cantankerous character led the local Tsonga people to bestow upon him the nickname 'Skukuza' – the one who turns everything upside down. The main camp of the Kruger National Park and the main airport are named in his honour. In fact, the administration offices of Skukuza Camp stand in the area where Stevenson-Hamilton settled his second, and permanent, camp while warden from 1902 to 1946.

Such was his dedication and commitment to this place, that it wasn't until he was 63 years old that he retired to White River and married a lady 34 years his junior before having three children and enjoying a family life in his later years.

In 1903, the area between the Sabie and Olifants rivers was added to the reserve, and by the end of 1903, the Shingwedzi Game Reserve was proclaimed, covering the area between the Letaba and Levuvhu rivers. The subsequent addition of further farms added to this vast protected area.

Meanwhile, the areas to the west of the southern part of the park had been surveyed and divided into 'farms' by a man named WH Gilfillan. He gave these pieces of land strangely European names like Toulon, Alicecot, Charleston, Exeter and Arathusa.

These farms were sold to various owners, both private individuals and companies such as the Transvaal Consolidated Land and Exploration Company.

The company used its properties for farming, but many of the private owners had their areas given over to leisure pursuits, such as winter hunting. Increasing private owners purchased land from the company in the mid to late 1920s, and they soon began to discuss putting together a private game reserve, which duly happened in 1934. The Sabi Private game reserve was born, which eventually became known as the Sabi Sand Game Reserve after the Second World War.

In 1961, the Kruger Park authorities, fearing the infestation of foot and mouth disease and the lack of control over the hunting activities in the area, erected a fence between the park and the private land to the west. This fence was more of a barrier to the movement of large ungulates and bigger game, but did nothing to curb the movement of predators or, to some degree, elephants, which simply pushed it over. It certainly had an effect on the movement of large numbers of animals, so when its removal was negotiated in 1993, it allowed wildlife to roam freely between the two areas again.

It is not too much of a stretch to say the dropping of the fences was a paradigm shift in the conservation history of South Africa and all of the famous game-viewing establishments that had been created in the Greater Kruger Park area were now truly contiguous with one of the world's great wildlife reserves.

Roughly from south to north, the major conservation areas and associations that make up the GKNP are as follows:

- Sabi Sand Nature Reserve
- MalaMala Game Reserve
- Manyeleti Game Reserve
- Kapama Private Game Reserve
- Thornybush Private Game Reserve
- Timbavati Private Nature Reserve
- Umbabat Private Nature Reserve
- Klaserie Private Nature Reserve
- Balule Game Reserve
- Letaba Ranch
- Makuya Nature Reserve

PRIVATE CONCESSIONS WITHIN THE KRUGER NATIONAL PARK

The concept of private concessions and lodges within Kruger National Park was born out of a need to offer exclusive and luxurious wildlife experiences while promoting sustainable tourism within the park.

By partnering with private entities, the government-run entities and parks boards could create a sort of public/private partnership that ushered in a new era in Kruger's history. Specialist hospitality operators introduced international standards of luxury and service to the infrastructure of the National Parks' teams and gained access to pristine wilderness areas with no public access.

This initiative aimed to balance conservation efforts with economic benefits, creating a model where high-end tourism boosted the income and profitability of the government's publicly funded model, and contributed directly to the operations of the park. These private concessions and lodges operate under strict regulations to maintain the park's ecological integrity. They are granted exclusive rights to conduct game drives, walking safaris and other activities within their designated areas. In return, a portion of their revenue is directed towards conservation projects and community development initiatives, fostering a symbiotic relationship between tourism and sustainability.

The concessions within Kruger National Park have been a resounding success, with numerous benefits to visitors, the park and its surrounding communities. They provide exclusivity and luxury, enhancing the safari experience and attracting discerning global travellers. The personalised service, expert guides and intimate settings ensure guests have a unique and memorable journey into the wild.

From a conservation perspective, the private concessions and lodges are crucial in preserving Kruger's natural resources. The revenue generated from tourism is reinvested into conservation projects, anti-poaching efforts and community development initiatives. This model supports the park's ecological integrity and provides economic opportunities for local communities, fostering a sense of ownership and stewardship.

One significant benefit of private concessions is their contribution to anti-poaching efforts. The presence of game-drive vehicles and the continuous movement of guests and guides throughout the concessions deter poachers. Frequent patrols and vigilant observation by safari guides help in the early detection of suspicious activities, thereby reducing the risk of poaching incidents.

Moreover, many private concessions have established dedicated anti-poaching units that tirelessly protect wildlife. These units have advanced technology and trained personnel who monitor the area, conduct patrols and respond to threats. The collaboration between these independent entities and Kruger National Park's authorities has significantly enhanced the overall security and protection of the park's wildlife.

By choosing to visit a private concession or lodge, travellers can enjoy an unparalleled safari experience, while contributing to the preservation of one of Africa's most iconic wilderness areas. The success of these concessions highlights the importance of sustainable tourism and its positive impact on both people and the planet.

These private concessions and lodges within Kruger National Park propose a unique and luxurious way to experience the beauty and wonder of the African wilderness. Each concession provides a distinct and unforgettable safari adventure. By supporting these private entities, visitors play a vital role in the conservation and sustainable development of Kruger National Park, ensuring its natural treasures are preserved for future generations to enjoy.

The concessions within the Kruger Park are:

- Camp Shawu
- Camp Shonga
- Hamilton's Tented Camp
- Hoyo Hoyo Lodge
- Jock Safari Lodge
- Imbali Lodge
- Kruger Shalati – The Train on the Bridge
- Lukimbi Safari Lodge
- Pafuri Tented Camp
- Rhino Walking Safaris
- Shishangeni
- Singita Lebombo Lodge
- Singita Sweni Lodge
- The Outpost
- Tinga Lodge – Lion Sands

SEASONS

The distinct seasonality of the annual cycle in the Greater Kruger Park offers different experiences and opportunities throughout the year. We are regularly asked about the best time of year to visit, and our answer is always the same: there is no bad time of the year to go on safari!

While this may sound like a general answer, it is absolutely true when you consider the different advantages of each time of year.

This is a place of extremes, where the two main seasons are determined by the arrival and departure of the rain.

The rainy season generally stretches from October through April, and it is a time of great abundance.

In late September, the day-time temperatures start to climb, and in the afternoons, thunderstorms build on the horizon, promising the advent of the rains ... but more often than not, they die out before delivering any appreciable precipitation. The bush almost vibrates in anticipation and even before the first rains fall, some trees and bushes are in bud and bloom. When the first rains do eventually arrive, the park becomes lush and green almost overnight as shoots of grass push through the previously parched earth, and trees and bushes become clothed in fresh green leaves. Waterholes begin to fill up and the landscape is dotted with shallow pools or 'pans'. River levels start to rise, and fresh water flows into the area from the mountain catchments in the Drakensberg to the west of the park.

For the animals that have made it through the dry season, this is a time of plenty, as food and water are readily available at almost every turn. Grazers such as wildebeest, buffalo, zebra and white rhinoceros quickly bulk up on all the fresh green grasses bursting through the soil. Browsers like kudu and giraffe have plenty of newly budded leaves and flowers to feed on, and generalists like elephant take full advantage of everything.

As the rainy season stretches into November, temperatures climb and humidity builds throughout the day, often culminating in dramatic thunderstorms in the afternoon and evenings. This can be a challenging time of year for game viewing, as the vegetation is much thicker, the water sources are spread far and wide, and the rain can interfere with game-drive plans but there are also some amazing benefits.

Firstly, the landscape with its lush greenery and dramatic skies make this the most scenically beautiful time of year; so, for photographers, there are great opportunities for breathtaking landscape shots with animals as subjects dwarfed by the scale of their habitat.

This is also the time of year when a lot of the antelope and plains game give birth to their young, and in the Greater Kruger Park, the most abundant antelope species, the impala, drop their lambs.

Impala are the iconic species of the park; so numerous that you tend to overlook them, but this graceful and beautiful antelope is a fascinating and integral part of all the interactions in this ecosystem.

Throughout the year, female impalas and their young live in what are known as breeding herds, which provide safety in numbers from the host of predators that feed on them – from lion and leopard, eagles and pythons, to cheetah, hyena, jackals and caracal, to name the main offenders. The more individuals there are in the herd, the lower the probability of any one animal falling victim to a predator. For this reason, impala herds often join with other bushveld species such as baboons, giraffe and zebra, each of which have specific advantages in detecting the presence of a skulking cat. The more eyes and ears at different levels and with different capabilities, the better the chances of an alarm ringing out and a hunt being foiled.

This vigilance, coupled with their incredible athleticism and reaction time to immediate danger, is one of the secrets to their success but there are a few more amazing aspects of impala life that contribute to this.

Impalas are in between the two general groupings of herbivores mentioned above; they are neither specialist browsers nor grazers but are able to feed on both leaves and grasses, giving them a massive advantage in the dry season and in drought years. Yet perhaps their most successful adaptive advantage is their breeding strategy.

Early in the year, when the rains are in full swing, adult male impalas experience a surge in testosterone, which drives them into the first phase of the breeding cycle of these remarkable animals. Their necks thicken noticeably with muscle and aggression soars. The bachelor herds they have lived in for the last few months begin to fracture, and the males vie to establish new territories. Prime real estate contains nutritious and plentiful food, and access to water and cover. Contestants chase each other and roar loudly as they do so, a distinctive sound of the bushveld at this time of year. Through February and March, competition intensifies; females are herded into whichever territory they happen to be passing through, and there are more serious clashes involving horn fights, which can, on occasion, prove fatal. In late April and early May, the rut peaks and mating begins.

Remarkably, all of the females in a particular area will be mated within a space of two or three weeks. While all this fighting and mating is taking place, dominant males will not feed or groom and rapidly lose condition. Not only does this allow them to only hold a territory for little more than a week before being ousted, but it also makes them vulnerable to predators, which zero in on all the audio clues that go with the rut. On numerous occasions, we have personally witnessed a leopard sneaking up to two fighting impala rams and killing one of them during the duel.

After all the fuss of the rut and mating season has died down, things settle and most males drift back to form loose associations in their bachelor herds. The gestation period is roughly 200 days – or six to seven months – and with the onset of the rains in November, the most remarkable and significant part of the impala breeding strategy occurs. Most of the lambs are dropped within two weeks of each other and in some herds, all drop within 48 hours. This has the effect of 'flooding the market' and, although the predators are tuned to the arrival of the lambs, they can kill only a relatively small number compared to the numbers available. The lambs that survive the first onslaught increase their chances of survival as they get faster and stronger by the day.

To get back to the advantages of the wet season in the park, it is this profusion of life with all the new arrivals that makes for superb viewing of the cuteness of the little ones, as well as the high incidence of predation and the increased possibility of seeing and photographing interactions between predators and prey.

Another huge benefit of the advent of the rains, and the warming day temperatures from September onwards, is the arrival of migratory birds from the north. It is estimated that nearly 4.5 billion birds make the journey from northern parts of the globe into Africa to escape the winter and stock up on food and improve their condition when they return to breed in the northern summer. Many of these birds arrive in South Africa through the course of September and October, and rangers and birders in the area always keep an eye open for the arrival of the first yellow-billed kites and Wahlberg's eagles, as well as for the trilling calls of the first woodland kingfishers – a sound that is ubiquitous and constant throughout the park in the summer months.

The rains generally come to an end towards late April and, by May, things dry up significantly and the dry season begins in earnest. Localised waterholes become parched and permanent rivers, such as the Sand River, attract more and more animals in search of water.

Days are cooler and predators – in particular, the cats, can be active during the day – ambush hunting along the river courses.

Large herds of elephants and buffalo are regular daily visitors to the rivers in their area and make for spectacular viewing as the dry season wears on. For example, buffaloes tend to drink twice a day and frequently have to travel fairly long distances from where they graze to favoured drinking spots on the river. Because of their exposure to predators, they prefer to move in fast, drink quickly and depart to a safe distance, where they rest and ruminate before carrying on with their normal feeding activity. The last rush to the water is often a mad dash, punctuated by bellows, frolicking calves and clouds of dust ... a photographer's dream.

The rivers and permanent waterholes become the focus of game viewing at this time of year and there is always something amazing worth waiting for in these areas.

The sunsets in the dry season are dramatic owing to the large amounts of dust in the air – and the frequent presence of smoke from wildfires – the nights are crisp and clear, the skies full and heavy with stars. This is indeed a magical time to be in this special place. With the advantage of being able to continue game viewing in the hours of darkness in the private areas of the GKNP, a whole new world opens up.

SAFETY IN NUMBERS

Well into the rainy season, large herds of grazing animals, like impala and wildebeest, are drawn to open areas where the grass has grown into thick lush lawns. This, of course, is also a magnet for predators, but the numbers of animals in the mixed species herds helps with the detection of any lurking danger.

LEOPARD ON LEOPARD

Wildlife photography out in the open during the rainy season is not easy – and seldom comfortable – although it does afford some wonderful opportunities to work with different lighting and conditions. The big cats are often active in the cooler conditions, and other species that remain dormant during the cold, dry winter become active, such as the leopard tortoise.

While following a young female leopard doing her rounds on the MalaMala Game Reserve, we were afforded the rare sighting of a leopard and a leopard tortoise crossing paths along a drenched game trail during an afternoon shower.

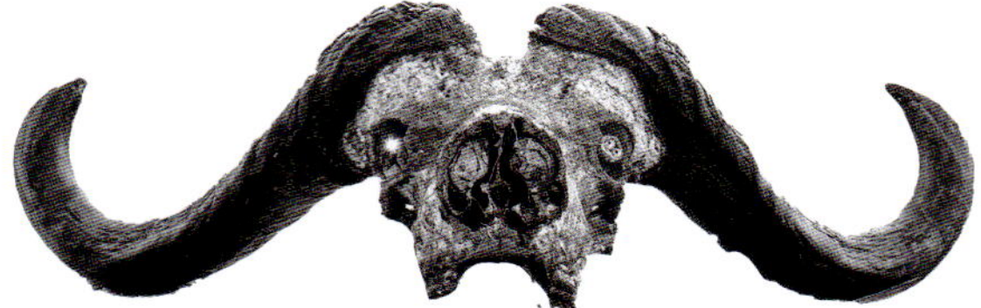

CLASH AT THE WATERHOLE

In late July, the Kruger Park dries up. In some cases, permanent rivers dwindle to mere trickles, and waterholes in the interior of the park rapidly shrink. Some spring-fed areas carry water throughout the dry season and these become magnets for many species of animals reliant on daily water. Buffaloes, for example, like to drink twice a day – usually in the late morning and early evening – and this can prove extremely dangerous for them.

In the northwestern reaches of the park, there are prides of lions that are specialised buffalo hunters, and at the end of the dry season, they almost exclusively hunt these dangerous customers where they come down to drink. We came across a pride of 15 lions camped out near a waterhole and noticed the great individual size of the animals, and the large number of sub-adult males in the pride. These were buffalo hunters for sure. On the way in, we had seen two or three large herds of buffalo moving across the parched landscape and were fairly certain this was going to be the right place to witness the ultimate interaction on the African savanna: lion versus buffalo.

As we sat there, the dust of a large herd appeared in the distance, and we heard the rumble of hooves and lowing of the buffalo as they approached. The first members of the herd came over the ridge above the waterhole and after a cursory glance around, descended towards the water. Excitement is always high when the thirsty animals get near and can smell the water; they break into a gallop to get in and start drinking immediately. It was late afternoon and the sun reflected through the dust as the herd arrived at the water's edge. We were sure they were aware of the lions but there was no choice. They had to drink and the risk was worth the reward. The lions stirred and formed on the eastern side of the waterhole. As the first buffalo splashed into the water, they charged into the fray. The herd scattered, bellowing and tossing their heads, but stayed close to the water. Some individuals went back in to drink, while the lions ran among them trying to pick a victim.

A male lion managed to grab a young calf, which bleated loudly, and a phalanx of buffalo bulls formed a line and charged to the rescue of the hapless calf. The lion released the calf and fled up the ridge while the bulls formed a protective circle around the calf until its mother returned to guide it towards to the safety of the herd.

While this was happening, a group of lions split to the west and charged in again. This time, they managed to grab an adult female buffalo. Again the protective bulls came to her aid, and chased off some of the attackers, but there were too many lions, and too much damage had already been done to the cow. The lions held on grimly as the bellowing buffalo was subdued, and the rest of the herd stood down as if realising that not much more could be done. In a cloud of dust, bellows and loud growls, it was soon over and the lions began feeding in a loud frenzy.

Remarkably, the buffalo herd did not retreat but moved around the waterhole and entered the water from the opposite bank to finish drinking before moving off, stopping every now and then to look back at the grim scene at the water's edge.

This was a dramatic clash between two of the most powerful adversaries of the bushveld. We were fully aware of how lucky we were to witness it but at the same time, we were taken aback by the lack of stealth needed by the lions, and the absence of evasion tactics by the buffalo. It was almost as if they knew they had to sacrifice one of their own to get to the water they could not survive without. While the herd numbered well above 500, this was obviously not a tactic that could work in the long term, and later that week – sure enough – the herd pushed on to the permanent rivers further north. (*Also see photo on page 4.*)

KING OF THE HILL

Dotted throughout the Kruger area are outcrops of granitic rock known as 'koppies'. These striking features of the landscape provide habitats and shelter for many bushveld species. Lions and leopards regularly use them as den sites for raising cubs, with lots of nooks and crannies to hide in, and a commanding view over the surrounding plains. Reptiles and snakes take refuge here and are frequently found basking on the rocks in the winter sun. Yet, the most iconic inhabitant of the koppie is the diminutive klipspringer, a name that literally translated from the Afrikaans means 'rock jumper'. These diminutive antelope are highly specialised for life on the rocks and spend their entire lives on and around koppies. They have soft pointed hooves that give them grip on the surface of the rock, and powerful hindquarters, which enable them to jump and leap about their habitat with amazing agility and poise. Scanning the rocks from afar and you might be lucky enough to spot a resident pair high atop their territorial outcrop. It is worth getting close and spending time observing their behaviour; they are great indicators of the presence of predators as they give a high wheezing whistle of an alarm call.

VIGILANT SENTRIES

The lurking danger of predators is a constant for almost all animal species in the bushveld. There is always something bigger and badder; either trying to eat you, chase you off or get rid of you as competition. Prey species are constantly vigilant and on the lookout for danger, and when a threat is detected, alarm calls ring out, warning others of the presence of a predator, and informing the predator itself that their presence has been detected and the element of surprise is eliminated. Rangers and trackers looking for big cats or other carnivores are tuned to the calls of antelope, birds and even other species of predator but their best friends and allies in this inter species communication are the primates. Vervet monkeys have a range of chattering calls that vary in pitch and intensity depending on the threat; snakes, birds of prey and smaller predators are chirped at in different ways, but the most intense and prolonged calls are saved for their prime nemesis, the leopard.

Baboons take this to the next level and should you hear the loud barks and screams of a baboon troop perched high up in trees, or atop rocks, you know they are looking directly at a threat. Just by following their gaze, you can often pick up on a leopard or lions.

DAWN'S DUEL ON THE LEADWOOD

The beginning of every game drive is an experience that never fails to excite, and a predawn start on a crisp and cold winter's morning in the bushveld somehow embodies the true essence of what a game drive should be. The smell of leadwood smoke still rising in the still air from last night's camp fire, the murmur of conversation of rangers and trackers with backs still turned to the last warmth of the fire, and the dawn chorus of a multitude of birds starting their day. As we got on to our vehicle and head out of camp, we were fully alert to sounds and signs – wondering what our first sighting would be, and what excitement lay ahead. Every day and each game drive is different, and one never knows if this will be a quiet and relaxing bumble through the bush – or an action-packed roller-coaster ride of dramatic experiences.

As the light crept into the eastern sky, we stopped at an elevated point to watch the soft pastel colours of a winter's dawn make their way onto the glowing canvas of the cool sky; lavenders, peach and soft oranges slowly revealed more intense golds as the sun begins to peep over the horizon. Coming from down in the river valley still clothed in wisps of mist, we heard that signature sound of a wild African morning – the low booming call of the African ground hornbill, 'Du du dudududu'. Such an evocative call that its name in the local Tsonga language is Nghutututu, and the Afrikaans name 'bromvoël' also alludes to the soft but powerful boom of the call.

Ground hornbills are usually found striding around in small family groups on grassy clearings in the bush, seeking out almost anything to eat, from snakes and frogs to mice, tortoises and insects. They

are large, heavy birds with huge bills and red faces and almost impossibly long eyelashes, and are a highly endangered species across their range.

Looking in the direction of the calls, Gerald spotted the large silhouettes of three ground hornbills in a stark multi-branched dead leadwood tree, potentially a dramatic setting for a great shot against the beautiful morning sky. We set off to try and capture the shot and as we approached the tree, we saw a fourth large bird on the branches across from the hornbills. To our amazement it was a martial eagle, the biggest of the African eagles and a fearsome predator. Their specific Latin name *bellicosus* translates to 'warlike', earned by their imperious look and aggressive nature.

It is amazing that even after years of experience and thousands of game drives, you suddenly realise you are looking at something extraordinary. Neither of us had ever experienced an interaction between these two species ... and what a show we were about to have. Gerald set to work with the cameras and readied himself as the action began to unfold.

As stately as they are on the ground, ground hornbills are awkward and uncomfortable in trees and are reluctant fliers. Suddenly, the attitude of the martial eagle changed and he fixed a steady glare on one of the hornbills before launching into the air and powerfully flapping towards the furthest bird. To our amazement, the hornbill stood its ground, pointing its heavy beak towards its attacker until the last minute before ducking swiftly out of the way of the eagle's outstretched talons and allowing its weight to drop to the ground before flapping heavily towards a thicket. As we watched in awe, the eagle had two or three further attempts at the remaining birds before giving up and flying off to another high vantage point.

We were left speechless at this incredible interaction. Gerald knew he had captured something special and unique – that great feeling that keeps the wildlife photographer coming back for more – along with the knowledge that each day raises the possibility of something you have never seen before. As we gathered ourselves, we heard the loud alarm barks of a kudu coming from the thick reed beds in the river. Off to the next adventure...

LEOPARD'S HIGH HAVEN

Contrary to popular belief, leopards do not spend a lot of time in trees but when they do, they take the art of comfort to new heights. The benefits of sleeping in trees are numerous: it is, as mentioned, quite comfortable; it is safe as there is little threat from other large predators; in the hot dry months, it is cooler and breezier aloft, and a refuge from biting insects; and it affords a vantage point to detect approaching danger or potential prey ... but only when that one heavily-lidded eye opens slowly to take it all in.

PRIDE DYNAMICS

Gerald and I have been lucky enough to observe, and spend time with, hundreds of different prides of lions throughout southern Africa over the last 30 years or so. One of the things we have learnt is a constant – there is no such thing as 'typical' lion behaviour.

Lion society revolves around the core unit of a group of related females who form the basis of the pride. They hold a territory that is passed down through generations of mothers and sisters, and these bloodlines can be traced back 50 or 60 years in some parts of the Greater Kruger.

Gerald recently spent the cycle of a year popping in to document happenings with a resident pride of lions when working out of Jock Safari Lodge, a concession within the Kruger National Park. They are known as the Windmill Pride and were in the midst of an upheaval during his early visits.

Here is part of his account of this time:

Two previously unrecorded male lions arrived in the area around Jock about a month after I started photographing here. They immediately began challenging the incumbent males by roaring and scent marking closer and closer to the boundaries of their territory. These two new lions were prime age brothers, both extremely large in stature and remarkably confident.

The ruling pair, a duo of seasoned veterans, had held their territory for over three years, but the newcomers were a definite threat. Soon the territorial posturing came down to physical encounters, and the previously dominant males decided to beat a retreat and disappeared eastwards, never to be seen again.

Quite often, these fights between ruling coalitions are solved in this way but occasionally they can be violent affairs where brutal battles can lead to the gruesome demise of the losers. These encounters are not so much over the geographical territory, but over the mating rights to the females in the pride. The tenure of male lions is sometimes brief, as there is constant pressure from other males, so they must mate with the females as quickly as they can to ensure their genes are passed on to the next generation. Unfortunately,

this can lead to the new males seeking out and killing any cubs that are present in the territory so that the females will come back into oestrus and be receptive to mating with the now dominant males.

As the two new males settled into their territory, a new struggle for dominance took place, this time between themselves! There were numerous skirmishes, which were more noise and bluster than anything else as they struggled over who was going to mate with which female first. They eventually sorted it out but I managed to capture some of the action, which was ongoing for a couple of weeks.

Seven months later, when I returned to the area, I was told two sets of cubs had been born to two of the pride females (one set was three months and the other set, four months old) but that they had been seen only a couple of times. On my first afternoon game drive, we staked out at the rocky outcrop where the cubs had previously been sighted, but there was no sign of the four females of the pride or the cubs. After a few hours wait, we eventually picked up some movement between the boulders and, one by one, a series of tiny faces appeared out of a crevice a little way from where we were stationed. Soon eight little cubs had emerged into the soft afternoon light to patiently await the return of their mothers.

As it turned out their patience was severely tested, as the lionesses did not return until the second evening of my vigil. For two days, I was treated to amazing sightings of the cubs in the early mornings and late afternoons as they continued the wait for their mothers to return. Lion cubs are programmed to be extremely stealthy and silent when on their own at a den site, but on the second afternoon when the lionesses returned, all bets were off and the cubs exploded out of the rocks in an excited ball of mewling, tumbling bodies as they greeted their mothers.

The lionesses were lean and clearly had not been successful on their hunt, or had been engaged in other activities, but they settled down to suckle and clean the cubs after the playing and greeting was over.

They spent the night and the next day with the cubs and during that time, the two new dominant males arrived and also made themselves at home. They had extremely full bellies, which led me to believe they may well have stolen whatever the lionesses had managed to kill and had followed them back to the den after a good feed on what must have been a rather large prey item. That night, around eight o'clock, the lionesses set off to hunt again, leaving the cubs under the watchful eyes of the males.

After the lionesses departed, they spotted an approaching male lion some distance away from the den. Three females quickly returned, while one lioness confronted the strange male. After a brief interaction, the male lay down where the confrontation occurred, and the female returned to the cubs.

The females were clearly uneasy but the two males remained oblivious to what had occurred out on the nearby plains as they slept off their meal. Later that evening, the females called to the cubs and moved them silently from the rocks to a nearby sandy riverbed where they made their way along the edges to a new den site, which we were only to discover a week later. It was apparent the females were still not comfortable with the new dominant males despite the cubs being their offspring and they were probably unsettled by the presence of another male. It turned out it must have been a young interloper moving through.

In one of those mysteries that are seldom solved, we discovered to our dismay that a young cubs was missing; he or she had obviously been lost or taken somewhere during the move and now only seven remained.

SPEEDY SIBLINGS

The burning amber eyes of two cheetah brothers are illuminated by the late afternoon light as they rest after a hunt. When cheetahs are seen together in groups, they are usually coalitions of related males, a mother with cubs, or a recently independent litter of siblings. It is always extremely exciting to come across these rare and beautiful cats.

TAKING TURNS

Vultures are always a great indicator of action in the bush. One day, while returning from a morning game drive out of Savanna Game Lodge in the Sabi Sand, we saw a large number of vultures descending towards an area of thick bush on top of a sandy ridge. We managed to find our way in there and came across a squabbling mass of well over a hundred vultures on what remained of an adult male impala carcass. As we set up to get some shots, a black-backed jackal came out of nowhere and rushed in to the fray, nipping at tail feathers and scattering birds as he tried to get a few bites of flesh from the rapidly disappearing feast.

He darted in and out, jaws nipping and tail sweeping back and forth, vultures cackled and squawked and hopped out the way, only to immediately return to the melee. As we snapped away trying to capture the action, another hulking shape appeared – a spotted hyena! Both vultures and jackal gave way to the larger, stronger scavenger, which promptly swooped up the carcass and, carrying it on high, made his way from the scene with his prize.

A NEW REIGN

It is always an anxious time in the bush when male lions take over a territory and drive away the previously dominant males to claim their new turf. If there are young cubs in any of the prides of females resident in the territory, they are generally the first casualties of a takeover.

The success of all animals in the wild and, in fact, all organisms on the planet is measured by the contribution of their genetic material into the next generation. All of the effort of reproductive strategies focus on this one measurement of success, and it is different in all creatures but in lions, it can manifest in violent and explosive periods.

Female prides are stable units and maintain territories in a relatively peaceful way by spacing themselves out in productive areas. Coalitions of – or sometimes single – male lions compete for territories that often contain multiple prides of females, with whom they will mate to produce their offspring. The benefit to the females is that they, and their cubs, are protected as long as those males are dominant. Sometimes male lions can hold territories for several years and successfully see multiple litters of cubs raised to maturity. Occasionally, their reign is short and unsuccessful and they are quickly usurped and their cubs killed.

A takeover usually begins when an invading coalition senses a weakness in the incumbent males, and begins a campaign of incursions into the territory signalling their intent. Patrolling and scent marking within territorial boundaries, roaring and advertising their presence, seeking out their intended target and physical altercations are generally the order of escalation. The incumbent males will either stand and fight, which frequently ends in violent and bloody encounters – often with mortalities – or they will turn tail and flee to fight another day leaving the path open to the invaders.

Before the new males begin to mark their new territory, their first order of business is to inspect all the female prides for new cubs, which they then mercilessly dispatch or chase off. The purpose of this is to bring the females immediately back into oestrus so they are receptive to mating. This ensures new cubs will be born quickly, and hopefully raised to maturity while they are still dominant in the territory.

This period is incredibly nerve wracking for observers and a pride we were monitoring out of Jock Safari Lodge had just undergone a takeover. New cubs had been born and the new males began threatening. We had not yet seen the cubs but on many nights, we heard the roaring and sounds of violent encounters between males, and feared the worst for the new cubs.

One morning on an early game drive, we tracked the females to the outcrop of rocks where we were fairly certain they had given birth, and were treated to the unbelievably moving sight of the baby lions tottering out of their hiding place in the crevices of granite onto a ledge for their first look at the world. We were privileged to be one of the first things they saw, and sat quietly in our game-viewing vehicle as they moved about on unsteady paws exploring their new world.

Underlying the beauty of this moment was the deep concern that the females were not present and the cubs were all on their own. With all the upheaval going on in the territory, had the cubs been abandoned to what would be a certain death? Had new males taken over and would they soon be here to finish off the vestiges of the last males rule? Had something happened to the mothers in the night?

We stayed as long as we could and staked out the den but even very late into the night, there was no sign of the females so we headed back to camp. Early the following morning, we were there at first light, and still the females had not appeared and the cubs seemed as anxious as we were. Perhaps that was just us projecting our feelings.

Finally in the early evening, we detected movement in the long grass and four lean and powerful figures emerged. They were home and safe, and there was no sign of invading males. We all heaved a sigh of relief, and spent the next three days around the den photographing the wonderful dynamics of the mothers and their new babies.

MAGNIFICENT MALES

The nyala (left) and kudu (above) are members of a family known as the spiral-horned antelope that occur throughout the Greater Kruger National Park.

Nyala are found mostly in the thick riverine forest on the banks of the major rivers of the park, and are an incredibly beautiful and interesting species. They display extreme sexual dimorphism, which means the males and females are different in appearance. Females are substantially smaller than males and a light rufous brown colour with 10 or more vertical white stripes down their sides. Males start off the same as females for their first year and then begin to change. Their coats become darker, the stripes fade and a set of spiral horns begins to grow. By the time they are fully mature, nyala bulls have a beautiful dark brown, almost black coat, and toffee-coloured legs, giving them the appearance of wearing plus-fours with a dark jacket.

Kudu are possibly the most magnificent of the region's antelope species; the males grow massive horns, which they carry regally as they move through their preferred thick woodland habitat.

Both species are secretive and quite elusive but nyala, in particular, can become fairly tame in the vicinity of lodges. During the dry season, they are regular, relaxed visitors that pay little heed to the movement around them when they visit to feed on the lawns and well-watered plants of established camps.

GROWING UP TOUGH

On Gerald's return to Jock after first seeing the new cubs of the Windmill Pride, he had numerous encounters with this growing band of youngsters. Here are extracts from his field notes:

On my return to Jock, seven months later, the cubs were approaching a year old.

Lion cubs grow quickly and, as always, I was amazed to see the transition from wobbly, playful little bundles of fur to young lions of considerable size and strength. Lions that could now compete at kills and move freely with the pride.

Cubs have to adapt quickly to rapidly changing phases of their life. They have to navigate the complexities of pride dynamics and learn to fend for themselves, while still being part of a team that has to work together. They must learn the behavioural intricacies of hunting as well as develop the physical strength and coordination required to take down large prey. A lot of this is done through play with siblings, while some is learnt from observation, and trial and error while the pride females hunt.

This latest chronicling of the life of a lion pride reinforces how grateful we are to have witnessed this same journey many times with different prides. Every story is different, populated by individual characters and interspersed with deep dramas, traumatic times and moments of tenderness, violence, triumph and tragedy. It is a privilege to witness nature in its true wild form.

The coming months for these youngsters will be critical as they continue to hone their hunting skills and social behaviours. The lionesses will gradually ease their support and become distant,

encouraging the cubs to be independent. The young males are still vulnerable to another pride takeover. At the very least, this could lead to them being chased off, but more than likely caught and killed by new males. The females may be safe from this and will join their mothers, split off as a splinter pride, emigrate to other prides nearby, or as happens in a few cases, set up shop on their own.

The private reserves and concessions of the Greater Kruger have afforded the ability for rangers and guests to spend extended periods of time with prides of lions and individual leopards on a daily basis, chronicling behaviour, family relationships, bloodlines and territoriality, for decades in the same areas. This has contributed enormously to our knowledge of the fabric of the lives of individual animals, as well as adding extremely valuable information to the scientific data base of these apex predators in a constantly threatened environment. All of this drives our understanding of how best to manage and protect the populations of all the animals that exist in extended conservation areas like the Kruger National Park, throughout Africa.

THE VANISHING SPEEDSTERS

Cheetahs are arguably the most highly adapted of all the world's large mammalian predators. They are made purely for speed, and everything else in their design and lifestyle revolves around this adaptation. To come across cheetah on a game drive is such a privilege, not only because they are few and far between and naturally widespread, but also because they are such exciting animals to spend time with. Unlike the other big cats of the Kruger, cheetahs are purely day-time hunters in open areas and very obvious ones at that. Once they move into an area, they are fairly easy to find as they are out and about during the day covering ground looking for prey. Cheetah have the habit of scouring the open plains from higher vantage points, often ascending to the top of termite mounds or into the lower limbs of trees to get a better view, especially in seasons when the grass is longer. Of course, as photographers, this is a stroke of luck as it makes them easier to find and wonderful subjects – often at a higher angle with lovely uncluttered backgrounds. However, as hunters, it does have some significant disadvantages.

Because they do what they do out in the open in front of anyone who is looking on, the prey species in the areas where they operate quickly become spooked. When cheetahs move into a particular area, their hunting success rate drops alarmingly within a couple of days, purely because all the prey species have become more vigilant after a couple of kills. Their obvious presence also alerts those canny scavengers, which sense a meal ticket in their neighbourhood. Hyena and jackals – and opportunistic leopards and lions

– can displace cheetah from prey with hardly a struggle. The ever-vigilant vulture is a constant threat as it alerts these other thieves to the presence of a kill. This makes life tough for the cheetah, a highly tuned and somewhat fragile speed machine. Hunting largely alone, a cheetah cannot afford to pick up an injury; even a broken toe can be a life-threatening situation for a creature so reliant on its athleticism. Any kind of confrontation with a more robust predator that may try to steal a kill is to be avoided, so kills are often abandoned and the cheetah moves on. They require huge areas of natural habitat to accommodate this lifestyle of constantly moving to new areas and that is one of the main issues in cheetah conservation, as it brings them into direct contact with human encroachment.

There are definitely signs that cheetah numbers are dropping alarmingly in most parts of Africa. Just from anecdotal evidence, it seems they are increasingly hard to find in Botswana where once they flourished, and in the Kruger area, sightings are a lot less predictable. Encroaching human pressure on habitat, low genetic diversity and all the other factors that tip the delicate balance of nature away from such a specialised animal, undoubtedly contribute to the situation, and the status of this magnificent cat is listed as Vulnerable on the IUCN red list. There are some excellent cheetah conservation organisations in southern Africa that deserve all the support we can give them to help protect this iconic species from extinction in the wild, which is unfortunately increasingly likely.

A LEOPARD'S TALE

Gerald and I have a long and happy association with MalaMala Game Reserve, and are fortunate to have worked at, or visited, this amazing place for nearly 40 years. During this time, we have grown deeply familiar with the area and the magnificent animals that inhabit it. With over 20 kilometres of the permanent Sand River running through this pristine wilderness – and the lowest density of guests to land in all of the GKNP – it is truly a wildlife haven.

We have seen the rise and fall of dynasties and bloodlines of lions, and the changes in populations of elephant and buffalo through years of drought and plenty. Yet more than anything, we have spent countless hours with generations of individual leopards. The Greater Kruger Park is the best area on the continent to view these magnificent, stealthy and beautiful cats. MalaMala, in particular, has a hot spot that is almost unbelievable in terms of the territories of female leopards it supports. This area, which straddles the Sand River, stretches from just north of MalaMala Main Camp to about two kilometres south of the camp and is currently part of the territory of at least eight female leopards.

The reason for the density here is a question of prime habitat. It has everything that female leopards look for: permanent water, riverine thickets, rocky outcrops and open grasslands. These different habitats allow for a wide variety and high concentration of prey as well as many ideal den sight options – a key factor in female leopard requirements.

A part-time occupant of the southern reaches is the Island Female leopard. As with many regularly observed leopards, she draws her name from the area where she was originally seen and most frequently observed, and has been the queen of this area for quite some time, almost a decade at the time of writing.

She is by some margin the biggest female in the area and arguably one of the most beautiful leopards we have ever seen. By any measure, she should be seen as a highly successful animal, except by that ultimate factor that determines the success of an animal in the wild ... their ability to ensure their genes are passed on to the next generation.

It is again the opportunities afforded by the private areas and concessions of the GKNP that allow rangers, visitors and researchers to witness and chronicle the intimate details of the lives of these magnificent wild creatures and so it is with us and the Island Female.

She was born in February 2013 and, as she grew, quickly became the favourite leopard to search out. When she had her first litter, rangers at MalaMala Game Reserve were excited that they were witnessing another dynasty of leopards emerging, but in 2019, rangers viewed helplessly as the Senegal Bush male killed her fourth recorded litter, a 13-month-old male cub. In early 2020, she had a fifth litter that was seen only a few times before they too disappeared, and so the morbid trend continued.

The litter of two cubs born in August 2020 looked like it might succumb to the same fate when the young male vanished at four months old. Despite the considerable odds stacked against her, the remaining female cub had a survivor's spirit and, at the time of writing, is now a two-year-old successful female that holds her own territory and displays remarkable hunting skills in and around the Matshapiri River.

Our journey with the Island Female has been more than just an observation of leopard behaviour and dynamics. Somehow she has become a portal into a world beyond our own – a connection to a deeper understanding of the wild and, in many ways, a muse.

Her desperate struggles to raise her cubs (unsuccessfully for the first seven years of her life) – juxtaposed with her high energy and innate playfulness when spending time with her youngsters – have played out like a show you cannot look away from. Gerald has enjoyed countless opportunities to photograph her and her interactions with her cubs, her environment and all the other creatures with which she shares her piece of the planet. She is the epitome of wildness, the ultimate individual of a special species. For this, we will be forever grateful.

With the success of her female cub, her legacy is secured after all these years.

In a wonderful footnote, in May of 2024, the rangers at MalaMala found two perfect little cubs tucked away in an outcrop of rocks in the Hogvaal donga, the Island Female's latest litter ... long may she reign!

THE CALL OF THE WILD

The African fish eagle is the iconic raptor of the inland and lakes of the continent. It is a large, stately bird with chocolate and black plumage, and a stark white head, ch Along the permanent rivers of the Greater Kruger Park, like the Sand, Sabie, Olifants, Timbavati and Shingwi can often spot these striking birds as a flash of white riverine tree.

They are well adapted to hunting their prey with mas and broad wings that allow them to swoop down on the generate powerful lift to remove large fish from under The ringing cry of their distinctive call is truly one o soundtracks of the African wild.

THE ELEPHANT CARCASS

Fires are an essential element of all of the Kruger Park habitats and part of the natural order and life cycles of all the complicated webs of the ecosystem. Fire regimes are managed carefully by all the national park and private reserve field teams but there is always the real danger of runaway fires that can consume huge swathes of bushveld in just a few days.

One such fire occurred while we were staying at Jock Safari Lodge in the Kruger Park, which sadly trapped and killed a sub-adult elephant. While his demise must have been one of terror and uncertainty, it happened quickly and the carcass was discovered the following day by rangers out on patrol.

It was an awfully stark scene when we arrived. The carcass was in a sandy river bed where the youngster had obviously tried to take refuge from the flames before succumbing to his wounds. The area was surrounded by charred grasslands that had been damped down by overnight rains and the smell of burnt vegetation hung in the air.

Over the next few days, this windfall of nutrition was to provide some excellent viewing and Gerald set up shop with his cameras to record the comings and goings.

As ever, the first of the big predators to appear were hyenas, which gave excited cackles and long whooping calls to alert other clan members to the sudden bonanza of food. The initial animals set about the difficult task of breaking through the thick tough skin of the elephant, using their powerful jaws and slicing carnassial teeth to cut away the softer parts and gain access to the underlying flesh. In the next few hours, the numbers of hyenas swelled and soon there was a cackling, shrieking, hellish scene of flesh, gore and snapping teeth as the clan squabbled over access to the entry holes into the carcass. As all this was unfolding, vultures arrived in great numbers, alighting on the bare branches of massive leadwood trees on the blackened surrounding plains. This, in turn, alerted other nearby scavengers and predators and we soon spotted the faces of a pride of lions peeking through the reedbeds on the sides of the river course. The hyenas were oblivious to the arrival of the lions, which silently closed in before rushing out of cover towards the mass of hyenas, scattering them and taking control of the feast. Hyenas slunk off to lie in the sand nearby, patiently waiting while the lions quickly filled their bellies.

As the lions moved off from the kill, one by one, hyenas opportunistically rushed in to claim some of the remaining scraps of flesh, bone and skin. Some of the lions half-heartedly gave chase but eventually flopped over in the shade to rest their huge bellies. Both hyenas and lions have the ability to gorge on huge amounts of meat at one sitting. In lions, the flesh is packed into a very expandable stomach. When full, it pushes upwards against the diaphragm and makes breathing difficult. For this reason, you may see lions lying flat on their sides around kills with their bellies bulging outwards, panting in short shallow breaths. Soon they start to roll over repeatedly, breaking up the contents and exposing more surface area to the incredibly powerful digestive enzymes in the stomach. Digestion is rapid and, within a day or two, the lions are restored back to lean, muscular athletes ready for their next meal.

HYENA HIJINKS

Hyenas hold an interesting space in the human psyche and are much maligned as evil, skulking, devious scavengers. They do fit that mould well but there is so much more to them and, when given the opportunity to observe social interactions in large groups, such as around a dead elephant, you may be rewarded with some pretty humorous and entertaining behaviour.

A large, decaying carcass is a perfect habitat for flies to breed en masse, and the swarms of these irritating insects at a kill are a source of great irritation to hyenas and lions. Lions often retreat to a distance in the shade during the heat of the day but hyenas need to stay close for fear of losing their place and have to engage in some hilarious gymnastics in an attempt to diminish the surface area exposed to biting insects and harsh sunlight.

SAY AAAH!

All cat species have highly developed tongues that play an essential role in many facets of their lives.

The tongues have hard outgrowths of skin projecting backwards towards the throat that give the entire surface of the tongue a rasp-like quality. This is extremely useful when grooming fur as it combs out loose hair, particles of meat and blood from feeding, parasites, as well as thorns and burrs that mat the fur. The tongue is also important during feeding, using it to clear fur from carcasses to allow access to incise the skin, and to grasp the last vestiges of soft flesh clinging to the bones of a kill.

As a wildlife photographer, the tongue of big cats is a wonderful, expressive and highly contrasting element in a picture. Understanding the behaviour of your subject, whether it be grooming, yawning or feeding, allows you to capture that critical moment when the seemingly impossibly long tongue is at full stretch, sometimes adding an amusing touch.

THE REMARKABLE JOURNEY OF THE RAVENSCOURT MALE

The Sabi Sand Nature Reserve is well known for its remarkable leopard viewing. Over more than half a decade, game rangers and trackers here have spent countless hours searching for, and spending time with, these magnificent creatures.

Leopards are naturally shy and their relationship with their human co-inhabitants of the savanna has been one of mistrust and evasion for millions of years. At first, these strange, upright-moving apes were part of their menu, which were hunted with stealth and guile, before the tables turned as man became the dominant species with his technology and cooperation. Leopards sunk back into the shadows and remained there, avoiding detection, competing for the same resources, which made them an enemy. In modern times, they were hunted mercilessly as vermin and then later as trophies for hunters seeking the thrill of the chase and the goal of bagging Africa's Big Five.

When game viewing started to become the focus of conservation efforts in the GKNP and hunting fell away as an activity, leopards remained elusive. At best, a flash sighting of a cat leaping from a tree or dashing across a bush road was all you could hope for. More understanding and sophisticated rules of engagement with leopards were instituted by private land owners and staff, and slowly the trust of a few individual female leopards was gained. As these animals raised cubs and game-viewing vehicles became a frequent part of their daily life, the population of relaxed leopards grew and we became used to the remarkable relationship we have with leopards in this special part of the world.

Over the last 50 years or so, there are countless tales of amazing individuals whose territories were known; their names became synonymous with special viewing experiences but perhaps none more so than the Ravenscourt male.

Ravenscourt is named for the property where he was first seen and grew up. At the time of writing, he is over 12 years old and still holding sway over a large territory in the northwestern sector of the Sabi Sand. Yet, even for an individual as legendary as he, time comes to an end, and he is slowly losing his grip to two or three younger males that are asserting their dominance in the area.

Ravenscourt has been spotted since he was approximately two months old. His mother was an extremely well-known territorial female, so he was seen often and his early years are well chronicled.

Only around one in six leopard cubs make it to a year old, and even then, they are not out of danger. This is when tragedy struck for Ravenscourt. His mother was protecting him from an aggressive male, which was taking over territory and trying to kill the yearling, when she was chased into a tree. She fell to the ground, broke her back and died. Ravenscourt fled. It was assumed he had little chance of survival, as male cubs tend to stay around their mothers until at least two years old before gaining independence and then spending a few years as a nomad trying to claim their own territory. Even with a good mother, these are extremely dangerous times for a leopard and no one expected to see too much more of the young cub.

Somehow Ravenscourt survived, however. He learnt to hunt and learnt to avoid danger in the form of lions and hyenas – and especially other leopards. He built guile and strength, and he slowly asserted his dominance in a densely populated leopard area. His rise was truly legendary and he has provided countless memories to thousands of safari-goers.

The last time Gerald and I spent time with him, he was doing truly remarkable Ravenscourt things. We found him with a fresh, massive male warthog kill one evening; a dangerous prey that takes a lot of skill, strength and determination to subdue. He had just finished feeding when he detected the presence of skulking hyenas. He grabbed the carcass by the scruff of the neck and hoisted it up the trunk of a nearby leadwood tree and continued his meal. The carcass weighed almost as much as he did; yet he did it effortlessly in another display of his prodigious strength and determination.

The following day we found him relaxing near a group of large buffalo bulls, which were not aware of his presence. We joked that, knowing Ravenscourt, he might be considering one of them as a meal. When the cantankerous old bulls finally realised he was there, they snorted and gathered together to seek him out. At this point, he departed with typical Ravenscourt nonchalance ... just fast enough to be safe, but not too quickly to lose the aura of coolness that makes him what he is: a legend.

TRUNKS

There is no mistaking an elephant for any other creature on the planet. Their massive size goes without saying, but it is the presence of the long prehensile trunk hanging from the front of their face that really gives them away. The trunk is a marvel of evolution, serving as a multipurpose appendage that has played a crucial role in the elephant family's extraordinary success through millennia. Essentially the trunk is a fusion of the elephant's upper lip and nose; a long, prehensile tube with two nostrils running down the centre, surrounded by a complex network of muscles, nerves, blood vessels and connective tissue. This intricate anatomy lends the trunk incredible dexterity and strength, making it a remarkably versatile tool for an animal of such immense size. The primary function of the trunk is to facilitate feeding and drinking. Elephants use their trunks to grasp vegetation during feeding or to suck up water and bring it to their mouths to drink. The trunk possesses over 40 000 muscles, providing remarkable agility and precision. It can lift massive objects, push over trees, easily rip off branches, but it is still delicate enough to pick up a single leaf or fruit.

BAOBAB – THE TREE OF LIFE

Baobab trees are a dominant feature of the landscape in the drier, northern regions of Kruger National Park. These majestic giants with their massive, gnarled trunks and distinctive twisted branches create a striking spectacle towering over the landscape.

The huge trunk of the baobab is made up of thick, fibrous, woody material that is able to absorb and store water to endure prolonged periods of drought. This has enabled them to survive harsh conditions and live for thousands of years, growing larger all the time. They truly are the tree of life, providing refuge and nourishment to myriad species; from massive elephants that strip and eat the bark, to tiny birds called mottled spinetails that roost almost exclusively in baobabs. Plenty of creatures use the baobab for shelter and leopards have been recorded raising cubs in cavities in baobabs. Baboons, genets, bushbabies and many other mammals spend time in their branches, and their flowers and fruits are not only consumed by animals, but are used by humans as food and medicine, having strong antioxidant properties.

SAVANNA SHOWDOWN

Game drives are an exceptional experience, even for grizzled old veterans of the bush who have been on literally thousands of them. The element of the unexpected is always lurking and extraordinary events can be triggered in the blink of an eye. On one morning drive, we had been watching and photographing a pride of lions feeding on a fresh buffalo kill when we opted to take a break and look for a leopard we heard was in a tree with a kill not too far away. We drove for about 10 minutes when we rounded a bend on the track and nearly ran into two huge male lions moving with purpose in the direction from which we had just come. This was an unexpected wrinkle for sure but what was more interesting was that they were not males we, or our ranger and tracker, recognised. Unknown males in an area always brings a sense of dread because there is so much that can happen in the lion population when this occurs. We made a snap decision to get back to the carcass as quickly as possible to set up and prepare. If these two intruders were headed for the carcass, there was some action to come.

The pride on the buffalo consisted of four adult females and some subadult males along with another set of younger cubs. There was the potential for a savage scene if these new males were taking over territory, so we sat in anticipation, and with no small measure of trepidation, while we awaited their arrival.

They took longer than we expected as they were clearly approaching with caution but our tracker soon spotted a male, his huge tawny bulk moving slowly towards us through the long backlit grass, head held high and nostrils flaring as he took in the scent and measure of the scene.

One of the lionesses sensed their approach and instantly, the three other adult lionesses jumped up from the kill and began growling warnings to the cubs. Everyone was momentarily caught in a still-life tableau as cubs watched their mothers, and their mothers sized up the males, which were also stock-still on the edge of the clearing with manes bristling and bulging muscles clenched as they leaned into the breeze coming their way.

The lead lioness suddenly made an unexpected move and charged powerfully towards the males, roaring and growling as she went. They were taken aback and a brief but incredibly violent and fierce engagement ensued. The cubs saw their chance and scattered. They fled into the surrounding long grass, while the other females moved into the fray, posturing and yowling at the unknown males. Although the males were outnumbered and a little surprised at the immediate engagement of the lionesses, they asserted their dominance and the females retreated a little distance and watched as the males trotted towards the carcass and began feeding, squabbling among themselves over the remains.

The fury of the vocal and violent skirmish was over. The lionesses had definitely lost the battle and their food but it seemed the war was only just beginning. They knew they were up against an unknown quantity and, having successfully defended their cubs, they decided to move quickly and as far as possible from the scene to assess their options. We had no idea where the incumbent males were and if this was a takeover. In a matter of minutes, our whole game drive, and the status quo in the lion community, was turned on its head. This is why you should never miss a game drive.

BAD HAIR DAY

The normally sleek and elegant grey heron (top) is caught in a bad-hair moment as it shakes its neck feathers after alighting at the top of a dead tree.

PRECISE EXTRACTION

An African harrier hawk (left) uses its specially adapted double-jointed legs to fish in crevices and holes in trees for nesting birds or mammals. In this case, it located a large gecko, using its beak to extract the lizard from it hiding place.

CLEAN-UP CREW

Oxpeckers are the most remarkable birds as they are wholly adapted to living their entire lives subsisting on food gleaned from their ungulate hosts, from medium-sized antelope and warthogs all the way up to rhinos and hippos. Their Afrikaans name 'renostervoël' directly translates to 'rhino bird'. They have short, strong legs with razor sharp claws on zgodactylous feet (two claws face forward and two back) and stiffened tail feathers that allow them to cling on and clamber about on their host's skin, even while moving at full speed. Strangely enough, elephants are not receptive to oxpeckers and actively brush them off with trunk or tail should they alight.

Their symbiotic relationship with their hosts is unique in the bird world, as they rely solely on ticks and other skin parasites, dry skin and flesh, and body fluids of their hosts to sustain them. While doing this, they serve as a clean-up crew to reduce the parasite load of their hosts, also cleaning wounds and eating scabs and fly larvae (maggots), which keeps the skin healthy and infection free. In comparison studies on impala in areas that do not have populations of oxpeckers and those that do, it has been determined that hosting oxpeckers reduces the need to groom, and the frequency thereof, by almost 40%.

The more common oxpecker species in the Kruger area is the red-billed, often seen moving in small family groups among herds of impala, buffalo and giraffe. Yellow-billed oxpeckers are far less common, and were in fact locally extinct until fairly recently.

Their unique specialisation nearly became their downfall when huge roaming herds of ungulates were exterminated by hunters in the 1800s, followed by the advent of cattle farming and arsenic-based dips to relieve the parasite loads on domestic livestock. Small populations of red-billed oxpeckers persisted in the Kruger and Zululand game reserves until more bird-friendly dips were introduced to certain parts of southern Africa and the birds could once again spread to farms and disperse that way. Efforts by concerned conservationists in Zimbabwe helped re-establish small populations of yellow-billed oxpeckers in the south of the country and, in the late 1970s, they naturally recolonised the Kruger through a strip of communal land from southern Zimbabwe. I can remember, even in the early '80s, being hugely excited when we would detect the presence of one of these birds among their smaller cousins, usually on big herds of buffalo.

Both species spend a large part of the day riding on their host animals, where they feed, mate, raise young and carry out all their daily activities while being ferried about to water when the animals drink, and to shade and shelter when the animals rest up. At sunset, they usually have roosting spots where they spend the night and when they are nesting, they lay their eggs in holes in trees, heading out during the day to join the others in their group on their vehicle of choice.

SPOTS OF SURVIVAL

Discovering a new den with young leopard cubs is an exciting moment for a wildlife photographer. The fact that leopards are so secretive and difficult to find – and because females become more evasive when bringing a new litter in to the world – makes this a moving and special event.

In the Greater Kruger, the selection of den site is a critical key to success for a mother leopard. The cubs must be well hidden and inaccessible to other predators. In other parts of Africa, den sites are really whatever is available; abandoned burrows in termite mounds, holes in trees, thick reedbeds and even old hamerkop nests have been recorded. Having spent many months in the area, it is almost always crevices or small caves in rocky outcrops covered in vegetation that do the trick; although, of late, there are more and more records of clever leopard mothers giving birth to, and raising cubs, under structures in the middle of safari lodges.

Here the cubs are born tiny and blind and completely dependent on their mother. She faces the dilemma of all solitary cats; she must nurture, protect and regularly suckle the cubs but she also needs to go out to hunt and feed. Lactation is extremely expensive in terms of energy required, so if anything, the mother has to increase her intake, which requires constant forays from the den. This poses two dangers; alerting other predators and scavengers to the den with her comings and goings, and leaving the cubs alone for extended periods of time where they are vulnerable to the same host of enemies. Lions and hyenas are the two obvious culprits, but they are also vulnerable to predation by birds of prey, jackals other leopards and African pythons.

As the cubs grow, they explore their immediate surroundings. They are playful, tumbling over one another in clumsy bouts of mock combat. Their spots, a mosaic of black rosettes against tawny fur, provide perfect camouflage amid the dappled light of the den site. This play is the beginning of their education in the business of killing, and leopards are the best in the business. They build their strength, hone their techniques and learn how to use their weapons effectively. Of course, this takes place only when there is a multiple litter but if there is a sole cub, the poor mother has to put up with all the energy of a growing, learning youngster. When there are two or more cubs, they may show different personalities from the beginning. Young males tend to be bold and adventurous, whereas females are usually shy and cautious.

As the cubs grow, so too does the range of their explorations. They venture out on short excursions, learning the nuances of their environment. They practise stealth and patience, essential skills for their survival. The cubs must learn to fend for themselves, to read the signs of danger, and to recognise the scent and signs of predators like lions and hyenas, which are constantly vigilant to the presence of competition.

The survival rate of leopard cubs is a grim statistic and most do not live past their first year.

Mothers will regularly move den sites once the cubs are mobile. They do this to escape the build up of scent and to ensure enemies are not alerted by constant activity at the den.

The cubs are now growing stronger, their senses sharpening, their instincts kicking in. They learn to climb trees, an essential skill for avoiding ground-based threats and for securing food. At around six months, the cubs are weaned and rely less on their mother for sustenance. They still depend on her for protection but they also start to hunt small prey on their own. Their play fights evolve into serious practice for the real struggles that lie ahead. Each day brings new challenges, and each night, new dangers.

As time marches on, the cubs approach the cusp of independence. At around 20 months, their mother's role as their protector and provider gradually diminishes. She begins to leave them alone for longer periods, forcing them to fend for themselves. The cubs wait patiently, their eyes scanning the horizon, watching and listening for signs of her return. During these times, they sharpen their hunting skills on smaller prey, their confidence growing with each successful catch. Mother will still lead them to her kills and allow them to feed, and protect them from other leopards should they cross paths.

This gradual weaning process continues and the cubs spend more time on their own. They learn to navigate the complexities of their environment without their mother's guidance. Each separation is a lesson in self-reliance, each reunion a brief respite in their journey towards independence.

Eventually the day comes when mother begins actively avoiding her cubs and aggressively chasing them away. Female cubs are usually ejected first as potential competition, while male cubs are frequently 'mummy's boys' and are allowed to hang around and reap the benefits of mothers hunting for a few more months. This is likely because they are bigger than mum and can bully her off kills, but by now the territorial male – often their father – will evict them rather forcefully.

Young females sometimes set up territory adjacent to their mothers, while young males face a period of being nomadic fugitives until they gain the strength and savvy to challenge for their own territories. The mother leopard seeks out the dominant male in her territory and is ready to mate and begin the whole cycle over again.

FASCINATING CREATURES

In the lush landscapes of Africa, a unique bond is forged between parents and their offspring. For baboons, nurturing and protecting their young is a testament to the depths of love and commitment within these social groups.

The entire troop rallies around the new arrival as soon as a baby baboon is born. Mothers and older female relatives quickly surround the infant, offering gentle nuzzles and reassuring coos. This communal care is crucial when the baby is most vulnerable during the first few weeks of life.

The troop's support extends beyond mere observation. Older baboons, particularly aunts and grandmothers, often take an active role in babysitting. They will carry the young ones on their backs, providing both transportation and a sense of security. This allows the mother to forage for food without worry, knowing her baby is safe and cared for.

As the African savanna transforms under the setting sun, a unique behaviour unfolds among the baboon population. These social primates, known for their agility and playfulness during the day, exhibit a remarkable change in their nocturnal habits.

Baboons have evolved to roost on high rocks or in trees for the night, a practice that offers both safety and rest. These natural platforms provide an elevated vantage point, allowing the baboons to survey the surrounding landscape for potential threats. The vantage points also offer protection from predators that may be active at night.

The silence of the African night is broken only by the occasional grunt or call from the roosting baboons. These vocalisations serve as a comforting chorus, connecting the group members and reinforcing their social bonds. As the first rays of dawn break over the horizon, the baboons will descend from their rock perches, ready to begin another day in the wild.

MOTHER LION

When mother lions return to a den full of active young cubs, there is always a joyous reunion and a period of intense bonding with the cubs. The little lions cannot get enough of the interactions with their mother, and compete with each other to vigorously rub heads and tumble all over the ever-patient female. This is an excellent time to get photographs of the tender side of lion life and patience is rewarded if you have the luxury of waiting for just such moments.

THE HORNS OF A DILEMMA

The future of rhino populations across the world – but particularly the two African species – is at a critical moment in a long history of dire situations, comebacks, successes and failures. The continued demand for wild rhino horn, largely driven by Asian markets, has rapidly increased as the economies of the main countries consuming horns grow and affluence of the individuals, who are willing to pay huge prices for even the smallest quantity, increases almost exponentially.

Poaching of rhinos on protected reserves and in national parks has reached epidemic proportions and, along with increasing populations, higher reward for horns and human encroachment into wilderness areas, things are once again on a knife's edge.

At the forefront of the struggle against poachers – and the monitoring and protection of viable rhino populations – are the anti-poaching units. On both state and private land, these units comprise of highly trained dedicated and incredibly brave individuals, who are on the ground and in the field, every day and night of the year. As the poachers and poaching syndicates become more sophisticated, and better armed and informed, this struggle to keep rhinos in the wild has become a war and it is playing out in the wilds of the Greater Kruger right now.

Many black and white rhino in the GKNP have been dehorned in a huge ongoing operation that seeks to diminish the chances of individuals being killed for their horn. Even tiny regrowth can lead to the animals being poached. The removal of horns can also prove fatal to rhinos in other ways; in particular, when territorial bulls clash and when females try to protect their calves against predators. This is not to mention that there is something unsettling about viewing a rhino in the wild without a horn, and how that impacts the sense of how wild these animals really are when we have to manage them in such a way. Speaking for ourselves, it is sad to see these magnificent creatures looking incomplete because of the necessity to protect them from our own species.

The reality is stark. The slaughter of rhinos for their horns will not cease until the demand for these products is eradicated. This is a simple economic principle. Suppliers will be willing to risk everything to meet the demand as long as there is a market. The solution, therefore, lies in education and awareness in the end markets. Consumers must understand that rhino horn, composed largely of keratin, presents no more medicinal value than chewing on their fingernails. However, changing ingrained cultural beliefs and practices has proved almost impossible and is not likely to gain any headway soon, so their protection in the field remains crucial.

There are two major schools of thought on the way forward in rhino conservation and, as with many of the efforts to conserve and protect iconic, charismatic species, there is no clear way to bring these two schools of thought together.

There are those who want an economic solution, positing that the only way to ensure the rhino's survival is to attach a monetary value to it. They advocate for the legalisation of the rhino horn trade and the private ownership of black rhinos, akin to the existing model for white rhinos. By doing so, they believe a controlled legal market and regulated trophy hunting could provide financial incentives for conservation efforts. This approach puts a tangible value on the rhino, hoping that this motivates private landowners and communities to invest in their protection.

On the other side of the debate, there are those who believe legalising rhino horn trade, even in limited deals, would prove disastrous as it has in other species historically. Also with the heightening demand and potential political instability throughout the rhinos' range, there is a massive threat of corruption with parties turning a blind eye to poaching. There is the belief that fostering a sense of stewardship and highlighting rhinos' ecological and cultural importance can lead to local communities with private partners and NGOs becoming the primary protectors of these animals. Tourism, in particular, offers a sustainable economic alternative, drawing international visitors eager to witness rhinos in their natural habitat, and generating the considerable amounts of money needed to protect them.

Another overarching need is for the wheels of justice to move swiftly and decisively in poaching cases. Too often, arrests do not end in convictions or if they do, sentencing is light and cases may be influenced by the poaching syndicates themselves.

Each side of the argument has pros and cons, but the path ahead is not clear-cut. The harsh reality is poaching syndicates are becoming increasingly sophisticated, outgunning and outmanoeuvring anti-poaching units. These units, while deeply committed, are frequently underfunded and understaffed, and face immense daily risks. They operate for long hours in harsh and dangerous environments, motivated by a profound commitment to saving these iconic animals. Their stories of courage and resilience are innumerable, and the job they do is immense but there is a constant demand for monetary support, equipment, technology, military and combat know-how, and top-end recruitment and training. There is also the deep need to get more community support and stop the infiltration of the very units designated to protecting the rhinos, from being infiltrated by elements within the community working for the poachers. It is literally warfare.

PURPLE HERON – THE PATIENT PREDATOR

Time spent at waterholes in the Kruger is seldom wasted. Even in the wet season, when there is little drama to punctuate the hot, thirsty days of the dry months, there is always something dramatic or beautiful happening, even if on a smaller scale.

The purple heron is one of the less common residents of water bodies in the area, but if seen, it is one of the more beautiful of the heron family, and a patient and deadly hunter. They are almost half the size of the formidable goliath heron but similarly coloured, so in the absence of side-by-side comparison, is sometimes misidentified by beginner birders. Another good way of telling them apart is the purple heron is often half hidden and secretive while the massive goliath heron has no problem standing proudly out in the open on sand bars in rivers, or on dam walls.

While taking a break at a waterhole during the heat of the day, we spied a purple heron stealthily setting up shop in a reed bed on the water's edge. A long period of motionless concentration ensued. Every now and then, the bird's head moved almost imperceptibly from side to side in a snake-like motion, used to judge distance to a potential prey item under the water. An incredibly fast strike followed and in a split second, a nice fat frog was firmly secured in the heron's bill. We watched him fishing for a few hours and frogs were his main prey, but their diet includes fish, small mammals and even some bird species.

WATERHOLE WATCH

The green-backed heron (above) is another wonderful bird to watch at waterholes. They have ingeniously developed the ability to use 'bait' to attract fish, and have been witnessed using spiders, insects, fruits or even feathers in this way, constantly placing and replacing the bait until a fish comes up and then striking with their bill and walking off with their catch.

Egyptian geese (right) are more common denizens, and almost every waterhole has a resident pair or two. They make their presence known with loud hissing and rasping calls, and frequent flight displays across the water while squabbling with other geese and any unlucky waterhole residents that get in the way.

HUNTING BUDDIES?

On numerous occasions we have come across packs of wild dogs that have hyenas moving with them. It is obvious the hyenas are there for a free meal, but it is remarkable how tolerant the dogs are of these obvious freeloaders. Some observations in the field seem to suggest there are individual hyenas that spend most of their time with wild dogs when they come through the area, and have an almost symbiotic relationship whereby the hyena adds to the packs defence when targeted by lions or leopards.

In all the cases we have seen, the relationship sours immediately a kill is made and the hyena is chased off with repeated attacks by the pack, involving numerous painful bites to the bum!

LEOPARD'S PREY

Leopards are known for having an incredibly diverse range of prey and everything from flying termites to mountain gorillas have been recorded in their diet. When we saw this large male leopard expertly catch a monitor lizard among the rocks on a morning drive, we agreed it was the first time we had witnessed this. He carried it triumphantly for a while but eventually dropped it. We expected him to settle down and feed but it was not to be. He sniffed it a couple of times, nudged it with his paw, and then strolled off leaving a perfectly good meal untouched.

It seems even leopards will draw the line at certain things.

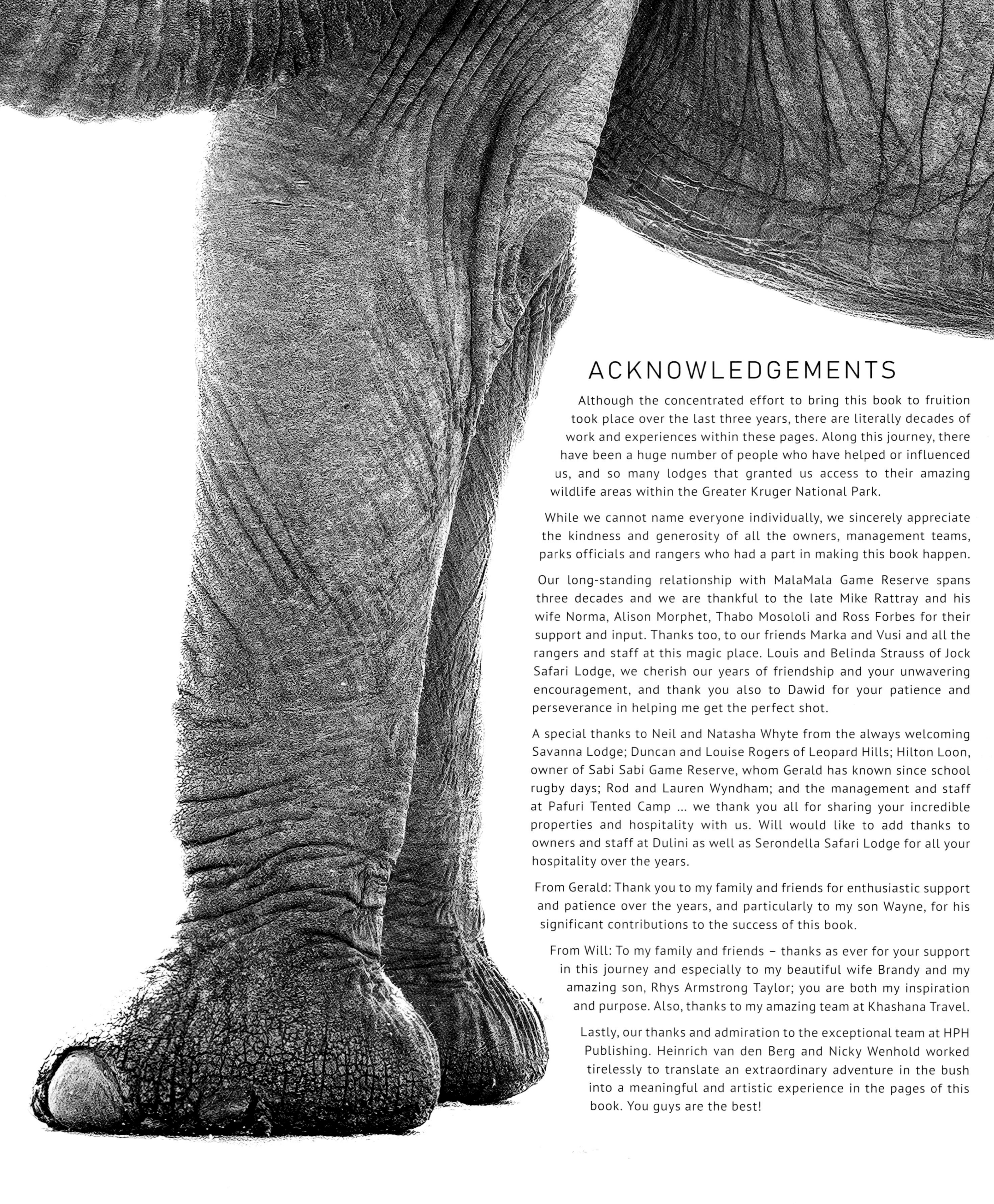

ACKNOWLEDGEMENTS

Although the concentrated effort to bring this book to fruition took place over the last three years, there are literally decades of work and experiences within these pages. Along this journey, there have been a huge number of people who have helped or influenced us, and so many lodges that granted us access to their amazing wildlife areas within the Greater Kruger National Park.

While we cannot name everyone individually, we sincerely appreciate the kindness and generosity of all the owners, management teams, parks officials and rangers who had a part in making this book happen.

Our long-standing relationship with MalaMala Game Reserve spans three decades and we are thankful to the late Mike Rattray and his wife Norma, Alison Morphet, Thabo Mosololi and Ross Forbes for their support and input. Thanks too, to our friends Marka and Vusi and all the rangers and staff at this magic place. Louis and Belinda Strauss of Jock Safari Lodge, we cherish our years of friendship and your unwavering encouragement, and thank you also to Dawid for your patience and perseverance in helping me get the perfect shot.

A special thanks to Neil and Natasha Whyte from the always welcoming Savanna Lodge; Duncan and Louise Rogers of Leopard Hills; Hilton Loon, owner of Sabi Sabi Game Reserve, whom Gerald has known since school rugby days; Rod and Lauren Wyndham; and the management and staff at Pafuri Tented Camp ... we thank you all for sharing your incredible properties and hospitality with us. Will would like to add thanks to owners and staff at Dulini as well as Serondella Safari Lodge for all your hospitality over the years.

From Gerald: Thank you to my family and friends for enthusiastic support and patience over the years, and particularly to my son Wayne, for his significant contributions to the success of this book.

From Will: To my family and friends – thanks as ever for your support in this journey and especially to my beautiful wife Brandy and my amazing son, Rhys Armstrong Taylor; you are both my inspiration and purpose. Also, thanks to my amazing team at Khashana Travel.

Lastly, our thanks and admiration to the exceptional team at HPH Publishing. Heinrich van den Berg and Nicky Wenhold worked tirelessly to translate an extraordinary adventure in the bush into a meaningful and artistic experience in the pages of this book. You guys are the best!

First Edition
ISBN 978-1-7764332-9-2
Text by Will Taylor and Gerald Hinde
Photography by Gerald Hinde
Publisher: Heinrich van den Berg
Edited and proofread by Margy Gibson
Design, typesetting and reproduction by
Nicky Wenhold and Heinrich van den Berg
Printed in China

First edition, first impression 2025
Published by **HPH Publishing**
50A Sixth Street, Linden, Johannesburg
2195, South Africa
www.hphpublishing.co.za
info@hphpublishing.co.za

HPH
Publishing